I0181150

Jigsaw

David Underdown

Cinnamon Press
:: small miracles from distinctive voices ::

Published by Cinnamon Press
www.cinnamonpress.com

The right of David Underdown to be identified as author of this work has been asserted by him in accordance with the Copyright, Designs and Patent Act, 1988. © 2022, David Underdown.
ISBN 978-1-78864-126-5

British Library Cataloguing in Publication Data. A CIP record for this book can be obtained from the British Library.

All rights reserved. No part of this publication may be reproduced, stored in a retrieval system, or transmitted in any form or by any means, electronic, mechanical, photocopying, recording or otherwise without the prior written permission of the publishers. This book may not be lent, hired out, resold or otherwise disposed of by way of trade in any form of binding or cover other than that in which it is published, without the prior consent of the publishers.

Designed and typeset in Bodoni by Cinnamon Press. Cover design by Adam Craig © Adam Craig. From original artwork: Torn paper illustration 86259060 © Fotoschab | Dreamstime.com

Cinnamon Press is represented by Inpress.

Acknowledgements

Some of these poems have appeared in *Snig* published by Calder Valley Poetry (2021). 'Mirror' appeared in the Wells Festival of Literature 2020 anthology and 'Notes on how to pack' was overall winner of the 2021 Wells Festival Open Poetry Competition and appeared in the festival anthology for that year. 'Furrow' and 'Two hundred and sixty feet' have appeared in *The High Window* and 'Audaubon encounters the American Avocet' in *Pennine Platform*.

David Underdown's poems have appeared in various anthologies and journals. His first two collections, *Time Lines* (2011) and *A Sense of North* (2019) were published by Cinnamon. *Snig* (2021) was published by Calder Valley Poetry. A Mancunian by birth, he spent the majority of his adult life in the West of Scotland including twenty years on the Isle of Arran. He now lives with his wife Claire in Hebden Bridge where he enjoys the deep valleys and Pennine moors and concentrates on walking, gardening, grand-children and writing poetry.

Contents

Psalm	9
Some things I cannot know	10
Still caught tight	11
Treecreeper in Crow Wood	12
Dipper	13
The pass	14
Woodpeckers in Falling Royd	15
Audaubon encounters the American Avocet	16
Apparition at the Booth Museum	17
The Potato Digger	18
A deceit of lapwings	19
Furrow	20
Sixth sense	21
The burying	22
Heart strings	23
My heart	24
More	25
Dream. Memory. Dream.	26
Two hundred and sixty feet	27
Passing voices	28
Ghosts might be like this	29
This house	30
Notes on how to pack	31
Her whole house inside out	32
She vows to withhold her secrets	33
Babushka doll	34
Night falls in the forest	35
Mind loop	36
(Not) dropping off	37
And afterwards	38
Fragment of a bas relief of the Final Judgement	39
Bone scan	40
Zugzwang	41
Torschlusspanik	42
Ancestry	43
Bristol Cream	44

Fragments from a Family Album

Impedimenta	47
Billy Goold 1921	48
Family group 1922	49
Scarlet fever 1925	50
Grandma Hallas 1927	51
Snap shot 1928	52
Newbiggin 1929	53
Sam 1931	54
1932: Puffin Patrol I	55
1932: Puffin Patrol II	56
Last summer 1933	57
9 St Peter's Rise 1934	58
Jean and Sylvia 1935	59
The weekend 1936	60
Wednesday Wheelers 1937	61
Weston-super-Mare 1938	62
The War	63
London 1951	64
The last summer	65
Mrs Bryant 1960	66
The mirror	67
Notes	69

Jigsaw

Psalm

1. I have swarmed with locusts and in the murmurations of starlings, woken snug within the pellet of an owl, stitched tight between the bones of mice.
2. I have followed secret runs to butcher stricken shrews and voles. My body bears stigmata from the octopus, the livid scars from razor clams.
3. Discharged from the guts of elk I was re-formed as winged beetle and jackal. I swallowed birds whole, have been spat out by sated dogs.
4. I was brother to plankton, and through the soft gauze of a moth's eye mapped the desert stars. I learned the ways of sturdy tardigrades.
5. Above salt lakes I skimmed in the gaping beaks of pelicans, on Ailsa Craig dived with gannets to snatch at silver.
6. For we are all of the dust of stars, hunter and hunted, reborn to soar splay-winged across the moon or shadow the lonely light of angler fish.

Some things I cannot know

On watching a tawny owl, Colden Clough, mid-morning. Wednesday 7th April 2021,

what you do for company
(out there in rustling darkness
a thin screech, fading)

whether you sense
the stirring wings
of others of your kind

the wiring behind those eyes:
how on its swivel neck
your CCTV monitors woodland traffic

what it is like to navigate
these branches splayed
across the starless dark

the taste of vole
badge of gore on your beak
(is that fur on your talons?)

owl-joy at the shriek of warm breath
as you bear it up
to your high
branches

to smell the colour of blood in the dark
its scent in the famished hours

and when your gizzard's crammed
is there an abatement to your restlessness?
What might it take to bring you peace?

Still caught tight

Kamikaze style he hit the glass beak first
and came off worse, broken neck probably,
a fledgling robin fresh from its nest;
and it was a reasonable request
to move the body from outside our door.
What stopped me? Less those shattered vertebrae
than an idea of a departed core, an unsung life
beneath its downiness. The watch unsprung.

Today, again, it caught my eye transformed
to a disassembled tracery. Bunched together,
claws, keel, metacarpals light as thought,
smudged feather, a minute orb of bone;
born of air and earth, warmed by blood, dispersed
yet there still, caught tight in my mind's net.

Treecreeper in Crow Wood

This morning I catch you
cantilevered halfway up
the oak's shady side.
It will have been
your umpteenth time today
and same as yesterday
glued to your bark
like a boy to his Nintendo.
Inch-by-inch you creep
your freckled back
turned against the light
to discourage chit-chat
from passers-by.
Ignoring distractions
of Spring and bird song
you poke your beak
in every crack.
O dainty Sisyphus
with your little scimitar
deft as a winkle-
eater's cocktail stick
you pick and probe
disturbing privacy
for countless bugs.
I wait to watch you
almost reach the sun
then flutter down
to try another tree
just like the last one.
It is your wit and talent
to peck and not be bored.
Starting over
is what you do.

Dipper

Finding you is like stealing
a secret. A hanging moment,
before, through dappled leaves,
you dart from sight.

Next time I am more wary,
skirting the hedge to catch you
in flagrante at the burn
intent on your obsession:
you study its silvered surface,
unblinking, awaiting
even a hint of perturbation.
As for me, I am not waiting:
time has stood still.
How can one so plump be so alert,
so two-faced, so drab and dazzling?
You turn your dowdy back
and puff your snowy chest:
it is as unnatural as an unpupilled eye.

Two days later you are there again,
the same place, your crisp white roundel
half hidden by foliage. I watch
until you sense my presence and are gone.

That's all. Just three times.
Yet now each time I pass
I look for where you were.

The pass

Fifteen years since I saw it,
moments imprinted on the sky
of my mind: the bird
swift from its kill
winging high from quartering
over the headland's bulk;
and now its mate,
a high-speed levitation from the moor
to make her somersault, mid-void.

Is this about a vole?
I see the instant of its drop
loosed from unfurled talons,
the seconds of free fall
to meet the mate's open claws
upturned to catch
and hold it tight again,
her stoop, faster than gravity
back to the ground-bound chicks.

That's all. Three seconds, maybe five,
victors and victim now long gone
but still a flip and snatch
in my brain's circuitry, a wonder
of black on white against the sky.

Woodpeckers in Falling Royd

We meet on a still morning,
me boot-deep in January mud,
your staccato rattle
breaking open silence.
Stop. And start again:
the randy percussion
somewhere up there
makes me laugh out loud
with joyful certainty
that good will come of it.

Still invisible you reverberate
a new branch
to tell us all
you mean business.
Down here, blind listener,
I am a captive audience.
I crane my neck to scan
each oak above the path
and catch at last
a scream of scarlet.

Your black and white
is topped and tailed,
crown and rump
as red as open wounds.
You batter the dead wood
to bring the woods to life.
And then you're off,
a streak of energy
that weaves past sleeping trunks,
your mate in top-priority pursuit.

Audaubon encounters the American Avocet

He's back in the reeds before daybreak, knee-deep for forty yards
to peep at her unheeding form three feet away.
Lovely bird! How innocent yet how near to thy admiring enemy!
She sits, head sunk, her eyes half closed, as if in dreams.
I have seen this, and I am content.

And yet the day previous unremarkable, through cottonwood scrub
until the first, glimpsed by the swamp, hovering and darting so far from ocean!
He can scarce believe their presence. They fill the field of his glass.
She balances head and neck, moving her head to and fro sideways
bill raking through soft mud.

The sketches: the male probing the waterline lower mandible thrust out.
Tongue emarginate at base. Beak to tail eighteen; wings thirty and a half;
intestine three foot six, diameter four twelfths. In a nest of woven grass:
four eggs, dull olive blotched with black. Plumage: exquisite,
rufous, even roseate, with hints of ash.

That night he dines on her. Bony, but passable eating, a transubstantiation:
aquatic worms and damsel flies to tender flesh. He surveys his plate,
its rim now lined with metatarsals, tibias, a scapula, a bluish claw.
Lately assembled for their adventure in flight, they are redundant now.
Replete, he sighs and wipes his mouth.

Apparition at the Booth Museum

Here you come, transported
through six generations to this dusty shed.
I smell the whisky on your breath
and hear your cut-glass words
spill on the floor like unstrung beads.
They roll to every corner of the room

where we are surrounded by chaffinches,
guillemots too, kestrels on crags,
and gulls, each shot and stuffed and set up in its case.
And I'm in shock: the bloodied eagles,
warblers snatched from grassy nests,
those gannet chicks you caged up in your yard
until their plumage changed; then killed.

What I will remember:
the silence as you puzzled to identify
the drone of traffic grinding up Dyke Road.
And how you arrived in the dusty vestibule
astonished by the woodlands' noiselessness,
the hedgerows of barbed wire,
the emptiness of open, open fields.

The Potato Digger

After Paul Henry

In the picture the shawl that cloaks you
is an artist's red that he has chosen to counter
the drab palette of the land where you stand
among ochres and the colours of dead grass.
It draws the eye like the girl in Don't Look Now
or Kubrick's film about the Holocaust.

If I was that spade you are leaning on
I would feel down my haft the weight of your weariness,
how you rest surrounded by clods
that you have cut and turned, cut and turned,
wresting a living from the sad land
of this beautiful island.

We, the onlookers, are resting too. Here in the gallery
we wonder if once you are done for the day
you might turn for a moment to look
past the low steading to the edge of the ocean
where your brothers left you behind. We marvel
at the deft conjuring of light from drab and red.

A deceit of lapwings

'the false lapwynge, ful of trecherye' *Geoffrey Chaucer*

Consider the shame of that name
even as they roller-coast over open skies,
over the secrets of ploughed fields,
keening and whooping to draw the farmhand on
away from their own open secret
nestled in its dark furrow.
See how she drags her uninjured wing
luring him from her little ones
as the boy with his bag counts his eggs,
and hatches in his mind
the money that will nestle in his purse.

Yet all over the down lands the skies are still thick
with the rush of their crossing, the thrum of their passing.

I know them by their secret names,
peewit, pie-wipe, chewit, tuefit,
the language of eggers and washmen and netters,
toppyup, peasiewheep, teewhuppo, thievnick,
telling their stories to tillers and ploughmen,
plivver, ticks-nicket, thievnig, peeweet.

And even now when a few come from nowhere
they are the sound of spring
a pied handful thrown against heaven,
the sky's calligraphy.
They swoop and tumble for the madness of it,
and cry, wheezy and slurred,
soft and wild, joyful and grieving.

I lean on my spade
and open my heart to their wing music,
watching their looping sky-dance
and how they play with the wind.

Furrow

I lean my whole weight on the spade
and slice its blade through claggy earth
until I feel the jolt of iron on iron.
And no, it is no treasure chest or Viking hoard
but, corny as a Christmas cracker, a horseshoe
to be cast aside. And back to the lunge of boot on lug,
the driving knee, the lift and swing.

I lean my whole weight on the spade
and see across the swell of grass
its history, the ploughman and his share:
the single blade that broke the ground,
the soil that rose and fell to a new straight furrow,
the hooves that drew the coulter on
along the Clydesdale's line of force.

I see that ploughman and his share,
his view across his great beast's massive rump,
its patient head that rose and fell to reach
the turn at stump or post and start again.
He would have set his line between its twitching ears
as through the sight of some great ordnance.
I pick the horse shoe up and feel its weight.

And clean the holes where nails slipped that day.
And hang it on my door, to keep my living straight.

Sixth sense

The frog's ancestral pool,
an eel's writhe and squirm
        to cross the ocean, beckoned
        by the Sargasso Sea's slow swirl,
and we too despite our preoccupations
        with children and libraries and online shopping
share this insistent itch
not needing the mystery of a word
        heimweh   *zugunruhe*
to feel the ruffling of the soul
        as now, in the unease that summons geese
        to gather at the waters' edge, the same shore
        where sand martins and house martins swoop
        engulfing in their beaks' gape
        every last midge or gnat,
        hearing the call to gather strength
        for journeys they cannot name,
we too feel the animal spark
undermine our equanimity
        the acrobat's hesitation
        almost imperceptible
        foot paused on air
        toe pointed to locate the line,
our fingers stretching for the bar of the trapeze
before it vanishes.

The burying

Down to the far corner we carried them,
you with the spade from the byre

like lees from two centuries
of all the lives lived in that house,
amassed on attic shelves, in cabinets and chests,
clogging corners of hallways and landings,

they were a harvest from the sea of faith at its full tide,
mindings of our unremembered lineage:
Aileen on the occasion of your christening April 1891…
Patrick for perfect attendance…
To my dear wife Constance…

The pile: in every conceivable size,
edges adorned with gold, chiselled
with finger-holds to find Leviticus,
Isaiah, Romans, Revelations. Psalms.

Covers: of stiff board, of plain cloth,
of leather dimpled with gilded lettering,
of faded velvet; but always black,
the universal blackness of deep space
save where bindings gaped like unhealed wounds.
Snagged pages revealed The Word.

Their smell: the scent of dead print, musty,
ingrained with dust that took your breath away.

The field: fertile, dark-earthed,
lush with spring grass and buttercups,
bound in by hedgerows of hazel and beech,
of holly and bryony.

And afterwards, our lightness:
the untelling of a secret,
the shedding of the heavy, unknown past.

Heart strings

I watched the father wait, the child wave,
the mother turn to go; and, like cats cradle
where you tug a thread and, struggling to untangle
what's been done, find somewhere else
a knot's been pulled so tight it won't undo,
I wept, not understanding what came over me.

Remember those contraptions with the wires
that stretch behind long panelled corridors
from rooms where people think they are in charge?
Someone yanks a cord and, far away
beyond the puller's hearing, a cacophony
of bells sets off an unseen pandemonium.

And today the scent of gorse on the breeze
and such joy. As if a lever in a signal box
has switched the points, our train's been side-tracked
to half-forgotten places: a welling over of the heart
where each familiar sound is ricocheted,
each colour so intense it burns.

My heart

wasn't left behind in San Francisco.
I take it everywhere, sometimes
in the wooden box where I keep special things
though sometimes in my day-sack for a walk
or, once, on a string like a rainbow balloon
that bobbed behind me in the breeze.

Someone I know buried his.
I would never do that. And though mine
might finish up in a trunk in the loft
I would rather share it with my friends
or even with strangers like the woman
I pass in the park with her dog.

My heart often has its own way
of doing things that my head does not agree with
which makes for arguments about taking life
seriously like signing petitions
or whether to become a vegan
or at least a proper vegetarian.

Then my heart has to take my head
for a brisk tramp over the moors
and give it a good talking to
so between them they can sort things out
and come back home, for that's
where it belongs, my heart.

More

She is the weather vane on the barn roof.
It spins with all that is inside her, welling up.
She can't look down without crying out
for more, the hunger in her head
as real as the rooks that wheel above the trees.
Her life was once an open sea
as unpredictable as each day's weather,
the colour of air in April, showers
shimmering to multiples of green,
yet today she is crying, *Save me! Save me!*
for the hope of something more than this.

And now Time is trying to get in.
It has pressed itself against the window
indignant when she tries to escape
to imagine her childhood Christmas Eves
and worry about the illnesses ahead.
Come here! it shouts. *Why don't you get a grip!*
There is tea on the table and look,
through that open doorway spears of hollyhocks
are blooming as if they've won first prize!
It's them that count. Forget the other ones
that used to grow, back then, behind your house!

Dream. Memory. Dream.

After Autumn *by Ali Smith*

It is a dream. It is a memory.
It is a dream of a memory.
It is Africa, hot, clear, young.
And a girl, looking down
from a lorry's open cab.

I am by the roadside looking up.
Her face is brown.
Her eyes are glinting.
She's amused.
Beside her in the cab is a goat.
She also looks down
through her goat eyes.
Their oblong pupils are indifferent
as blanked out screens.

I am by the roadside
for this is also a parting.
It is occurring to me
that I am falling in love
and in my dreamed memory
snatched in that instant,
I know that this is all
that will ever happen:
the girl, Africa, the eyes,
her mocking smile.

Two hundred and sixty feet

Over the years there must have been hundreds
but the one I saw, just one thank god, lives on
in mental debris trawled up today
by no more than a few words from a book.
She lies still where she fell
on that morning I saw her sprawled
across the mud of the retreating tide.

Spreadeagled, legs all wrong, her body
harnessed gravity but lost its proper shape.
At thirty-two feet per second per second
she fell through half a furlong of air.
Think of it in cricket pitches or the breadth of motorways.
Think how ground sped up as she dropped
past wooded cliffs and hulks of boats.

Looking down, her arms outstretched
as if to save herself, she would not see
Brunel's fine towers framed against the sky.
Did she hesitate? Was there a hopeless cry
for help that did not come, or was her short flight
silent, like a photograph, black and white
and never in the family album?

She was the first dead body I had seen
and half a lifetime later I am hoping
I am not the only one to wonder;
whether in a quiet moment
there is someone to imagine
the grandchildren who never came.
Or telling a child *you had an auntie once.*

Passing voices

Here at the open window silence
is frosted over by a faint beginning,
a conversation, voices heard
only by their music. Unseen,
speaker and listener explain and respond
like leaves rustled to life by breeze,
the warm give and take of small stories;
and somewhere else, the distant labour
of a diesel toiling up the Keighley Road,
a chatter of jackdaws from three gardens off.

The brief instant of passing:
a face and shoulders rear beyond the wall,
speaker oblivious, intent on his moment,
then sounds recede, sink lower, disappear.
Something like ghosts can nudge unbidden
thoughts like this of loved ones or strangers,
dispersed, their real selves long gone,
but shadows lingering on beyond the window
conjured now by no more than staying still.
And once, urgent, as if his presence could not wait.

Ghosts might be like this

A man once lost his senses,
waking beyond hearing
but apprehending within his head,
a heavenly tinnitus,
the rapturous murmur of a million tiny birds
filtered by light years.

Clapping, he heard no noise
save beyond the air beneath the sea
lugworms and tube-worms
writhing in the silent sand
and molluscs stretching feathery tongues
to catch small creatures.

His senses sloughed off one by one—
the scent of apples, the sweetness of milk,
the tightness of clasped fingers—
each peeled away and he
was not empty but overflowing,
blessed by the murmured music in his mind.

In his final blindness
he encountered the unfelt contours
of all his unseen surroundings
and lay beneath the stars
knowing precisely the immensity of each,
knowing precisely each fleck of starlight on his face,

could count them photon by photon.
And knew that ghosts might be like this,
like a speck of light,
like a chink in the blank wall,
like a tiny reverberation
more insistent than the rest.

This house

Staying at home so long this house
of weathered wood and millstone grit
its slopes and angles turning to windows

and stairs to rooms between beams
the line of the moors that tells
each morning all we need to know

what else could I wish for this house

the garden the forget-me-nots
so blue you fall past them each morning
the same morning as yesterday

living like the turning of pages
over and over not even trying
to search for photographs

and always I thought this

was our house I thought when we came
this is where we might live in these quiet rooms
for so many summers this house

built ochre stone by ochre stone
the one I long for the line of the moors
much closer than I thought

when we came here this was where

I thought there would be no going back
or forward I thought that this house
was where we would dwell

our blood and flesh and bone
with stories to tell one another
without asking why.

Notes on how to pack

You may be leaving, but that van, those cases
cannot take it all, so choose with care:
the table where you sometimes see their faces
from all those years ago, the rocking chair.

You cannot take it all, so choose with care:
the bed of course for its loving and grieving.
From all those years ago, the rocking chair,
but not the leaky tap. And chuck the sofa. Heaving

the bed downstairs, keep it for loving and grieving.
That corner window? Leave it with the creaking stair,
the leaky tap. And chuck the sofa, heaving
at the stink from when those mice had babies there.

That corner window? Leave it with the creaking stair.
Pack all the books, although you know
the mice have nibbled some. Who knows where
you'll store the milk jugs and that vase with its green glow

but pack all the books, although you know
you'll never find the day to read Ivan Denisovich.
Bring the milk jugs and that vase with its green glow
but leave behind the year when she fell sick.

You'll never find the day to read Ivan Denisovich.
For god's sake leave the strimmer!
And leave behind the year when she fell sick.
The piano is a shame, but take the sea, its shimmer.

For god's sake leave the strimmer!
No laughing matter to shed the best of all your days.
The piano is a shame, but take the sea, its shimmer:
past and future travel separate ways.

No laughing matter to shed the best of all your days
but you're leaving with the van and all those cases.
Past and future travel separate ways
so take the table where you sometimes see their faces.

Her whole house inside out

She says it is like the abolition of secrets
her house in Brierley Close at Number 10
as if there was a tremendous morning yawn
and stretch and then a crack no more than a hair
all down the front by the bay window
a wavy line that crept from underground
up to the roof
                    and she will never forget
that unsteadying and the sound
of a rush of air like someone with their lungs
already full and trying to inhale
ribs cracking and beams and timbers
and shattered glass
                              and when the building broke
how it flaunted its fabric for the world
to see inside the sitting room the stains
around the bath and the ducks still up the wall
the noise that was wheezy a belly laugh now
with chimney pots falling like angels
and plumbing bursting into open air.

Strangest of all, she says, when the hush came
like a pause for breath on the stairs
her house was there but inside out
as if it had been flayed and made again.

And now the world can see the way she lives
the wardrobe doors spilling her dresses
and last night's tights strewn across the floor
and she, she says, with nowhere left to turn.

She vows to withhold her secrets

I will not tell you my secrets:
the one about my brother's wife;
the one about my niece;
the one about the man in the house with no key.
I will not tell you how long they have been mine
or who else might know.

Think of them as stones that as years passed
have piled up, and under each
the thing that must never be told.

You will never know their shape,
or their scent, or whether they glitter;
if they are like boulders, or grains of sand;
if some are too heavy to lift
or others glow in my palm
like pebbles washed smooth by the sea.

Babushka doll

A summer night, late June, July,
with yesterday still fading in the milky next-day dawn
and somewhere out beyond the open window Miles Davis
lazy-fingered, sifted through warm air
to me, in this street, in this house, in this room,
in this bed, awake, imagining my other lives,
Miranda in her brave new world.

Night falls in the forest

First the trees. Feel their trunks.
Imagine you can reach and touch
their boughs, their branches, leaves.
You see them through your fingertips.
We say they are pitch black.

Up there beyond the trees is sky.
The blankest shapes, the ones like fuzzy-felt,
are clouds. Often they are all there is
but this evening they have holes
and through the holes a different sort of black,
liquid, oily, viscous,
and strewn with distant windows.
It is a glimpse beyond the edge.
This is the universe. It is everywhere.

And tonight for an hour or two
another mystery: a flawed face swimming
smirched by light lost to shadow.
If you could rise, drawn by the finest thread,
to share its pale presence
you would be illuminated.

Listen, now there are sounds too.
They crawl and cling and prowl, blind
but stealthy, determined to make progress.
Wait for the snap of a twig
or the stumble of a foot on a root.
We call this fear.

Mind loop

Out in that open boat
unsheltered from the squalls
that night has summoned up,
the nearest land's a mile away
through water that's so cold
I know I would not last.
My only hope's to stand
and hang from the precarious mast
to find the line of lights.

And if, like squirming down a telescope,
I can zoom in to spot the window,
yellow lamplight on the fireplace wall,
the chair, the empty cup,
I'll find myself again, imagining
the lonely boat out there.

(Not) dropping off

The mind has its compass
so perhaps there is more to it than letting go,
patrolling tunnels trip-wired by afterthoughts,
to where the sink-hole waits.
If real chemistry is going on it must be here
where signals in the brain's Hadron Collider
ricochet and counter-spin,
a Corryvreckan of the soul—
with no end to it.
Night drags and fidgets, wide-eyed,
black as a board, spiked with thorns.

The mind has its compass
so perhaps there is no more to it than letting go,
traipsing tunnels after thoughts as deep as trees
to where the sink-hole waits.
If real chemistry is going on it must be here
where signals elide down passageways,
neurons settle into patterns,
a gentle peristalsis to oblivion—
and at the end,
night snuggles down, heady-scented,
close as the blanket, studded with pearls.

And afterwards

'Just old truth dawning: there is no next-time-round.' Seamus Heaney

This morning she described an afterlife
not in the sky but here where we are now
and as if we are in love, not frenzied
but subsumed by all the small particulars
of whatever life we have led. *And then,*
she said, *a gathering up*, meaning a moment
as when those earthy graves that Spenser painted
burst wide, spilling people, in their prime
and overjoyed to see the sun again,
alive to its warmth upon their resurrected skin.

But I'd say this, that as death comes we lie
like those I once saw at the burning ghat,
lined side by side and tightly wrapped in cloth
to wait their turn; and knowing that our winding cloths
are fabric we have woven for ourselves:
coarse and patched, or close knit, braided,
plain or nubbly, drab or dyed
with berries or rare pigments
in purple, ochre, pearl, incarnadine.
And some, shot through with glinting filaments.

Fragment of a bas relief of the Final Judgement

The monsters are not fierce. Eating people
is what they do. There is no malice
in the one that already has encircled
the sinner and soon will tear out his throat.
And the other? It has come between his legs.
Its scales scratch the soft skin of his thigh.
In a minute it will consume his manhood.

As if he is asleep, the man does not resist.
The sculptor knows this not as possibility
but fact. He has carved the idea in marble
that is cool and drained of all colour,
polished smooth. The hard work of making
is past and his labour done.
This is how it will be. It is set in stone.

Bone scan

Waiting today I'm thinking of bones,
you setting off for school, elbows and shins,
the narrowness between your skeleton and skin.
You hang like a coat on its hanger.
Those bones of yours.

And now, flapping from the handlebars, your bag
has sandwiched between wheel and fork.
It is, you say, the only time you've flown,
the air, the sky, you hurtling through
and landing winded, all your bones splayed out.
You would not move for fear: your foot,
your body, still joined, but in between
a dark place you had no mind for.
You lay and wondered what would happen next.

We're finding out: the screen, your archaeology,
the doctor tracing fracture lines, new, old,
the dark places that are up to no good.

Zugzwang

At last the afternoon is theirs. They find the board again
and sink into their favourite chairs.
Through the window she can smell the flower beds.
His usual start, Sicilian, unless it is that bluff of his…
When they first met she'd swear he sometimes let her win
but that was fifty years ago. Now he enjoys the fight and knows
she can more than hold her own. She loves to watch him think,
head bowed above the board like in their London days.
How thin his hair is now, and white.
Still in the game she bides her time.

Outside, the border is past its best, starting to sprawl,
but asters and anemones are in their pomp. Salvia too.
The after-play. Though she should have tidied up the lupins.
He takes her knight and glances up, pleased with his move.
Odd he should sacrifice the rook. The sun is skulking behind cloud,
breeze ruffles the pages of her book. He has no way back now.
She reaches for her cardigan. Goose bumps.
On family holidays in France they used to call them *chair de poule.*
White queen's bishop to c4. Zugzwang.
It will be back-rank mate. Soon she will suggest a pot of tea.

Torschlusspanik

Beneath his collar night bites colder.
The moon is in its last quarter.
The howling edges nearer.
His knees have turned to water.

The last time he will lift up a child.
The last day he will swim in the sea.
The last summer to pick apples.
His last dram.

The howling edges nearer.
His knees have turned to water.
Somewhere out there it is waiting
as the short days grow still shorter.

The last bet he will lose at cards.
His last passport.
The last morning of making love.
His last ride on a train.

Somewhere out there it is waiting
as the short days grow still shorter.
The barking's become louder.
He fears that he will falter.

The last sunrise.
The last lie he will tell.
The last storm in the night.
His last promise.

The barking's become louder.
He knows he must not falter
though night's cold beneath his collar
and the noose is even tauter.

Ancestry

What was the discontent about
(or was it vanity that led me on)
to send my DNA, the spitting image of me,
across an ocean to a foreign lab?
It was not merely idle curiosity,

but more the thrill of maybe being someone else:
an absurd idea that my cherubic mouth
(so mocked at school as blubber-lips)
and my Bristolian mum's unruly hair
might have a flashier tale to tell.

My fantasy? To put the two together
and make three, an untold story I could tell
to prove a differentness I felt I felt:
that I was more than ordinary me,
that someone stranger must have crossed my path.

The mundane truth came back. It left no room
for doubt that after all I'm from a single place,
a place I've tried but never managed to escape.
My chagrin makes me laugh, to see my straight
straightforwardness, my undiluted me.

Bristol Cream

A hand-breadth high, tapered,
they catch the light through angled surfaces,
rims etched with trailing vines,
a tiny bunch of grapes between each leaf.

Too late to check, but I think you bought them
when you moved and had more space:
two glasses to have Sunday sherry in,
one for you and one for him.

On visits later when it was just you
I'd fish them out and find the Bristol Cream
to try to help your feeling blue.
And soon it was a habit, what we'd always do.

I have them here. Held to the light
their facets break the room apart
and re-assemble it, scattering planes
of this week's tulips on the table top.

And today, a silent toast: to you,
refracted beyond the window
where in the garden's splintered jungle
you've gone to catch the sun.

Fragments from a Family Album

Impedimenta

The suitcase when I found it in the loft
was ghastly tartan with a broken zip,
the first receptacle to come to hand
the day the clearance van arrived
and time ran out (as it ran out for you).
I must have shovelled everything inside,
all the relics there was no time to sort,
the stuff that someone thought to tuck away
because it hadn't yet been finished with.
Jumbled in amongst the letters and the cards
were photographs, blurry, black and white.
I tipped them out. It felt like rifling through
a stranger's pockets, or walking round a town
I'd heard about but never visited.

Billy Goold 1921

Let's call her Meg. He doted on that spaniel
and this is their usual stop by the grassy bank.
He has her by the collar. Not that she would ever run away:
if dogs could smile she would be smiling,
enveloped by her favourite male smells.

He is in his flannels, lace-up boots, a woolly tie, and today
a bowler hat! Its brim in the sun is a flourish of light.
Behind, an oak casts impenetrable shade.
No smile. Right now his attention is all for Meg.
Her tongue lolls. Her eyes are only for him.

And this one, same spot, just a different angle,
and he is back in his flat cap. She is on her haunches,
paws raised for a biscuit. She drools for him to let it drop
so she can catch it as she always does
and he will pat her haunch and say *good girl.*

I cannot hear if his Bristol burr is tempered by an Irish lilt.
There is so much mystery about his woman's world:
Ida, Meg, then Phyllis and now Isabel.
That faint shadow on the road is Ida.
She will be waiting while Meg scoffs her biscuit.

Family group 1922

They are in their heyday, Billy with tash and cap,
togged up in his three-piece and shiny brogues.
He is remembering to hold his shoulders back
while Ida is relaxed, slender in a calf-length skirt.
She looks more fun than I remember in her later years.
Her hat with its ribbon shouts high summer.

Between them at the front is Phyl, eight years old,
bare-foot, a short white dress and rolled-up sleeves.
Holding their pose the grown-ups have no hands for her
so she clutches her mum's skirt and a fold of his trousers,
fingers tight around a bunch of each of them.
They are looking straight ahead. They have just said cheese.

Isabel is only two and on the rocks behind.
We just see her top half, above her dad's shoulder.
Her shock of still-blond hair is all over the place
and makes a halo in the sun. Back there
is much more interesting than the grown-ups.
She has discovered a world of her own.

Scarlet fever 1925

No one thought to take a photo of this,
but imagine. It's Wednesday early closing,
the shop is shut, so Mrs C has brought you over
just to keep you quiet. Your sister is in bed,
still not allowed to get up, but your mum
heard the bell and came downstairs.

She is the other side of the glass door,
and I don't know how many times you've been told
she can't come out, but it's still not fair.
From the other side of the door she is waving
and you, you are weeping. Your mouth and hands
leave smears all down the glass and she
is only mouthing words you cannot hear.
Come on, says Mrs C, *you'll catch your death.*

Grandma Hallas 1927

Family legend says she was the mill-owner's daughter
who married the millhand and was cut adrift.
Her mother sewed six sovereigns into the seam of her coat.
Ten children, and a reputation:
you always claimed she frightened you to death.

Today she looks the part: she could be Grandma Addams.
You have stopped at a five-bar gate by a beech hedge.
Beyond is a gimcrack chalet with a flimsy roof
but flimsy is no word to use about Grandma in full regalia.
She stands like a man, crow-black, heavy limbed,
and her coat has room for two, lapels like donkeys' ears.
She is planted on the ground as if she's been installed.

Am I unfair to see her like the ogress you described?
Not by the look of Pugsley and Wednesday either side.
You are on the gate, unruly ringlets bursting from your hat
and if looks could kill that pout of yours would clear the field.
You well deserve to have your knuckles rapped.
Phyl, in her teens, is examining her nails
a yard or two back, weary for the performance to finish.
She is hoping she will catch the eye of a passing lad.
But there will be no sovereigns for either of you.

Snap shot 1928

It's 1928, but none of the big world matters
for you two are making your own world here,
just you and your dad and the dog.

The dog waits patiently as cocker spaniels do.
Billy is in his suit and cap, collar nicely starched
but there is nothing starchy about him today

sprawled back with one leg on the bench.
And you, nine years old, are as pleased as can be
in your short white frock and grown-up shoes.

You've pulled a chair across so you can lean
into the crook of his shoulder. Your hands
are clasped around your chubby knees.

Nobody cares that your knickers are showing,
it's just a great laugh, you and your dad
while mum and big sister are home at the shop.

If there is such a thing as bliss this must be it,
this hour or two, just you and him. You are laughing
as he tells a yarn from his childhood in County Cork.

You are laughing, but not at the story.
Above your heads you watch late sun stream in
without a thought for what might lie ahead.

Newbiggin 1929

I think it happened by The Cut,
though you never told me what, or why
you had a twitch, touched lampposts and the like;
only that you went to stay with Uncle George and Lily.
The change might help you act less strange.

And here you are, on a seaside golf course
thick with flowers, oxeye daisies,
maybe rattle or squill. You don't look twitchy.
Just a half set of clubs, though you're hardly high enough
to stop the bag from dragging on the ground.

Like a podgy sentry with your rifle
you clasp the strap, arm dangling at your side.
You are looking right at him and holding onto your smile.
I am wondering whether there is a question:
Am I doing this right?

You're right enough. Your pleated skirt
has ridden up and shows your dimpled knees.
Your shoulder tilts against the weight of the clubs
that have tugged at your shirt
and pulled it tight across your tummy.

Plimsols, no socks and that smile
that may just be for the camera,
it's hard to tell. Perhaps the sun is in your eyes.
With this wind, by the time you're home
your hair will be a right tangle.

Ninety years ago, you, and your uncle after work
making the most of a summer evening.
The cell with half of me is already there inside you.
It will need to wait another sixteen years
but that is not what's on your mind.

Sam 1931

No puzzle about the girl. It's my mum.
She's down the road by The New Cut.

She's twelve years old and horsing around
pretending to read a grown-up newspaper.

And isn't the phone box great
with its mahogany and enamel sign?

Him? His name is Sam.
He was in the First World War.

And was lucky, for years later
here he is trying to eat the newspaper.

He stretches out across the rail.
She can smell his breath, feel his mane.

1932: Puffin Patrol I

The bell tent needs its sturdy ropes
to cope with these strapping guides.
Brown Owl (who is amazing by the way)
and her six girls are all crammed in
and looking out from the flappy doorway.
The brailings make a skirt around their knees.
Inside at night they say their prayers,
sleep feet to pole, spokes of the same wheel.
Thoughts spin at all that lies ahead.
But this morning they are wide awake
ready for the time of their lives.

1932: Puffin Patrol II

What a laugh, the pair of you,
you and the girl with the glasses.
I think her name was Mabel.
You're in your uniform, behind her,
body bent to the length of hers,
arms late-summer brown in those short sleeves.
Someone, perhaps it was Brown Owl,
has trussed the two of you together
with an enormous corset! It encircles you.
Redundant suspenders dangle round your thighs.
Mabel is thirteen too, skinny as a rake
and somehow I would say she's not so sure.

Last summer 1933

For Billy Goold (1886-1933)

The writing on the back is dithery
but it's mum's all right, and just says 'Daddy'.
This must be the year it happened.
It's a hot August day on the coast
and he has stripped down to his braces.
We can see the garters holding up his sleeves.
He is perched on a hillock for the snap
and not taking any chances with the sun
with those boots and woolly socks.

Ida will be thankful she thought to take it.
That shadow with the hat is her.
Billy is man-spreading and as pleased as punch,
big hands clasped around each knee.
His mood is as expansive as his waistline.
He is eyeing Ida. You can't tell what's been said
but perhaps it was to find his hat:
I never realised that he was so bald.

In just four months that tooth will flare up
and the infection will sweep him away.

9 St Peter's Rise 1934

It was, mum says, the first of the moves,
ten in as many years: new school,
new friends to try to make.
It's a semi, what we'd call 'pre-war',
but no one knew about that yet.
They must have been almost giving them away:
a lifetime later she could still tell me
that the deposit was only ten pounds
with a free turkey thrown in.
Bay windowed, Snowcem over brick,
the front door at the side for privacy
and Ida stands alone on the cement path,
dark skirt, no smile and looking older.
He has been dead six months. Not much
in the garden. No one else around.

Jean and Sylvia 1935

The gulls are out of sight but you can hear them
in battalions, arguing across the salty sands.
Flat as a spread-out tablecloth below a mud-grey sky
the Bristol Channel's effort at a wave has been caught in the act
of lapping, falling over itself half-heartedly
to edge its turbid water on another foot or two.

The photographer's right elbow has tilted the horizon
so the coast of Wales runs uphill from left to right
and yet the water does not run away, it idles
as if it is waiting for something to happen.
And, layered across these horizontals, two sisters
stand with bony ankles in the sea.

The one in shorts is twelve, high-summer brown.
She is poking a net at what is probably a crab.
Her legs cast gawky reflections on the wobbles of the sea
and I can't explain why, but I think this may be
the very moment she turns from tomboy to young woman:
you can sense the pressure of the gathering sap.

Her big sister is a naiad, bare legged, loose-limbed.
She is trying to be interested in the crab but has no wish to touch it,
and has goosebumps. Her fingers clench against the chill,
knees flexing as she bends towards the younger girl.
She would like to suggest that it's time to go in
but knows that this will make her feel mean.

Someone has seen the unspoken gravity here: the sisters,
the empty beach, the cords that hold them, their eggshell-frail love.
She orders a reprint and adds a sticker that says
Merry Xmas instead of what she is really thinking:
the pair of them with no need for words
to say they will always be there, the one for the other.

The weekend 1936

Minehead. It's summer, just a long weekend
but special for you sisters, the two of you
stepping out past the bowling club
on one of those broad, clean-swept pavements.

It must have been a year when everyone
was wearing headscarves and hems below the knee.
She shimmies like a model on a catwalk, and you
are longing for another inch or so to flounce your dress.

This afternoon she is setting the pace
hands clasped around that smart handbag
so you have tucked your arm under hers
and are trying hard to keep in step.

The two swells follow at a decent distance
in baggy, double-breasted suits.
They have just clocked the pair of you.
They are quickening their pace.

There's the prospect of banter. After all
you're all on holiday. What larks you will have.

Wednesday Wheelers 1937

If bikes were horses yours would be Clydesdale mares.
You have stopped at the end of the alley in your short-sleeved frocks.
Wednesday, your favourite day, and a pause for a snap.

There are flowers everywhere and soon you'll be bowling along
past Shepton Mallet to Wookey Hole and Glastonbury.
Last week was out through Blagdon to the Mendip Hills.

Once on the road, the tongue-tied boys
will forge on past the giggling centre of the pack
to show their sturdy calves and well-turned bums.

And later under the apple trees, lettuce sandwiches
and horseplay from the lads that will have Mrs P fizzing.
She's half a mind, she'll say, to send for Mr P to sort them out.

When Ken from haberdashery saw you'd grazed your knee
he made you stop to bathe it in a stream. Your mind still raced
after he'd seen you home. That night he kissed his handkerchief.

You never knew.

Weston-super-Mare 1938

It could have been a bit of a laugh
three girls at the seaside, the free weekend
at Mrs Mackie's B & B, no beaux,
no ties, no family looking on,
the ride out from the city
with saucy waves to idlers and gawpers.

A fine spell too, deckchairs
like a dormitory along the prom,
sun worshippers, brown and white
and Neapolitan pink, suffering their pleasure.
Families cluster round their bathing huts
and down by the canoes the young men josh.

Kodak in hand you must have run ahead
and snapped your friends mid-step.
The one on the left looks up for some fun:
skimpy jumper showing off her curves,
sunglasses like magic X-ray eyes,
cherry lips and sassy smile.

But there's no doubt who's leading lady:
short skirt, haltered top,
bare knees and shoulders;
a face to launch a thousand ships,
she holds the camera's gaze
and lets its unlying eye size her up.

And eighty years on I am wondering
how the weekend went,
and when that wonder woman,
snapped on a cloudless day
daring the taker to take her,
would blink.

The War

It is the only one of you together.
Cornwall, 1940, your honeymoon,
and you have borrowed a dog,
a spaniel just like your dad's, and a boat
beached on the shingle. You are in the stern
arm-in-arm with the dog on your lap.
It was a day when the sun was shining.

Otherwise they are all of you in your costume
in the shallows, or on a rock pretending to dive,
or this man in baggy clothes who will be my father.
He has his shirt off to skim stones,
and here he is by the harbour wall,
hands in pockets, head inclined, always serious.
You know you can trust this man.

In London afterwards you write to your best friend
about the wedding, nights in the shelter and dogfights over Kent.
Nothing of the honeymoon, just how different life is now.
I know from your stories there was time in Wales
but not a single picture for the next six years.

And then this house in Manchester.
The pram in the garden like a boat on wheels.
There is a baby propped inside.
It is me. It is 1947.
The hardest winter in living memory.

London 1951

My first time in London, South Bank,
the Festival of Britain. Down the road
King George will be in his Buckingham Palace

though here is a bit like a football ground
with lots of concrete, a crowd in the distance
that could be a queue, and only the odd passer-by.

Dad is taking a snap while it's quiet but no one is cooperating.
Ida has come dressed for winter in her beret
and the thick stockings we borrow to put out for Santa.

You are taking no notice, looking up at all the modernity
in a blouse that shows off your brown arms; and that's me
in school shorts and braces, wondering why we have stopped.

The futuristic pole held up by wires is functionless,
but this is the future. It is going to be much better
than the past. We are here, waiting for it to begin.

The last summer

For Phyllis Mead (1914-1959)

The haymaking has already started:
summer is slipping by too fast
so he snuck off early from the office
to suggest a surprise drive, just to get some air.
He has stopped the Hillman on this quiet road.
The Kodak in its case was on the back seat
so I think that the idea of the picture
was in his mind all along.

She's in the frock that lately has become too big.
Its folds catch shadows from the sinking sun
that fall in furrows from her waist.
Her necklace seems too heavy for her neck
but she is smiling for him the smile she has learned
helps a man to put his best foot forward,
and he will be smiling back, steadying his hands
against the bonnet of the car.

The haymakers have gone home to their families
and left the trailer with the bales half-loaded.
With her 1950s perm she smiles for him
and what he sees is how handsome she looks
now her cheekbones show and her arms as thin as a girl's.
Her fingers twine a strand of grass like worry beads
but she can look straight at him for they both know
the truth even though it has never been spoken.

Early evening sun has transformed the scene:
in another story we might be set for an alien abduction
but in this one she is waiting, foreground, left-centre,
the empty field behind. Over her head
a luminous bank of cloud is hemmed in either side
by space so dark and deep it must go on for ever.
Above, the wires hum on their roadside pole.
They are carrying power away to who knows where.

Mrs Bryant 1960

This picture, the only one of you I have,
tallies with the woman I remember
as the mum of my mum's best friend.
Bundled up in a sensible coat and bucket hat
I cannot imagine you turning heads.
It looks as if a moment later
we will catch you rummaging in your handbag.

For me, you were never anything but old.
If I had ever stopped to think I would have said
that while you fumbled with the buttons of your coat
life passed you by. And yet who is this
tucked in the corner of the frame in black and white?
You have cut around the edge of his uniform
to keep him separate from his other concerns.

And for these few minutes I will bring you two to life,
face to face, and you, Mrs Bryant, in your young skin.
Yes, let him for one more time encircle
your unbundled waist so you feel again
the strength of his arms, just as so often
through those later years you tried to summon him.
He will keep you as safe as he can.

The mirror

For Isabel Underdown (1919-2014)

For years it seems you must have been
in black and white, hiding down in Cornwall
in tiny photographs, or up in Llandudno
or cooking those Sunday-dinners-with-Yorkshire
that so often seemed to end in tears

but then you bought brushes and pastels
and shared that summer stall through festival week.
Those framed Cotswold churches snug in their villages
gave us no warning of the years to come
after you'd discovered *everything is light.*

It was all about colour you said, though the jugs
and bowls of fruit you brought to wonky life
never prepared us for the mirror, and how
for a year or more you turned yourself inside out
in paint on canvases you did not show your family.

Stacked up, in that bedroom studio
where your heart had gone to live, were life-size heads
in slabs of paint there was no arguing with.
You didn't give a fig they weren't for hanging
in the sitting room, or what we'd do with them

and afterwards they gazed at us for months
defying all our plans to clear the house.
I have one still, on the hall wall
held in its place by landscapes either side,
though I know it was never all about colour.

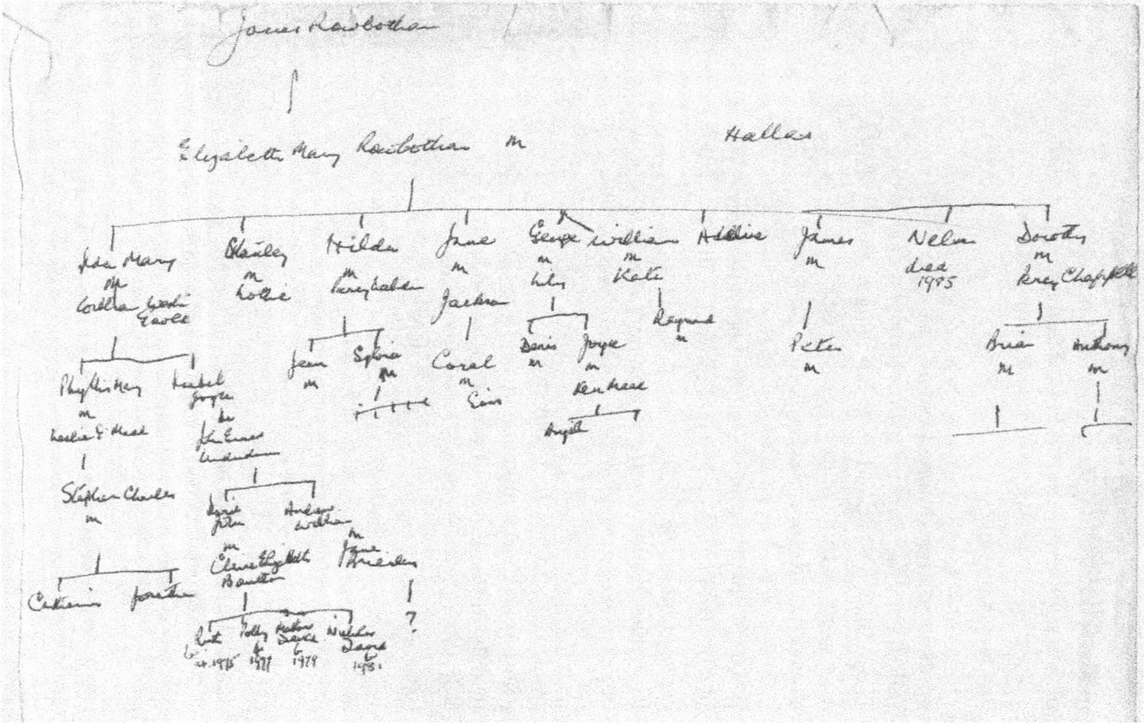
Elizabeth Mary
m
Hallas
Ida Mary
Stanley
Hilda
Jane
George
William
James
Dorothy
died 1995
Lottie
Jackson
Lily
Kate
Raymond
Peter
Jean
Sylvia
Coral
Doris
Joyce
Brian
Anthony
Phyllis Mary
Isabel Joyce
Stephen Charles
Catherine
Jonathan
?

Notes

Apparition at the Booth Museum:

Edward Booth (1840-90) devoted his life to creating dioramas to show every species of British bird in its natural habitat. They are housed in the Booth Museum in Brighton.

Fragments from a Family Album

My mother, Isabel Joyce Goold, was born in February 1919. Just before the Covid 19 pandemic I began a much delayed final clear-out of her things and came across a small suitcase of unsorted photographs. A few were familiar, but most were new to me.

Finding them made me realise how little I knew about her life or the lives of my grandparents. These poems are a response to some of those largely unannotated images. Apart from 'Mrs Bryant' all the people mentioned appear on a family tree compiled by my father shortly before he died in 2003.

www.ingramcontent.com/pod-product-compliance
Lightning Source LLC
LaVergne TN
LVHW041309080426
835510LV00009B/922
* 9 7 8 1 7 8 8 6 4 1 2 6 5 *